Gelato!

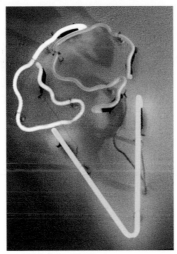

Gelato!

ITALIAN ICE CREAMS, SORBETTI & GRANITE

TEXT & RECIPES BY PAMELA SHELDON JOHNS

PRODUCED BY JENNIFER BARRY DESIGN

PHOTOGRAPHY BY JOYCE OUDKERK-POOL

TEN SPEED PRESS

BERKELEY • TORONTO

A Kirsty Melville Book

Ten Speed Press
Box 7123, Berkeley, California 94707
www.tenspeed.com

Distributed in Australia by Simon & Schuster Australia, in Canada by Ten Speed Press Canada,
in New Zealand by Southern Publishing Group, in South Africa by Real Books, in Southeast Asia
by Berkeley Books, and in the United Kingdom and Europe by Airlift Books.

Concept and Design: Jennifer Barry Design, Sausalito, California
Production Assistant: Kristen Wurz
Copy Editor: Carolyn Miller
Food Stylist: Pouké
Prop Stylist: Carol Hacker/Tableprop

Library of Congress Cataloging-in-Publication Data
Johns, Pamela Sheldon.
Gelato! : Italian ice creams, sorbetti & granite / text & recipes by Pamela Sheldon Johns;
produced by Jennifer Barry Design; photography by Joyce Oudkerk-Pool.
     p.   cm.
Includes index.
ISBN 1-58008-197-5 (cloth)
1. Ice cream, ices, etc.   I. Title
TX795.J64   2000
641.8'62--dc21   00-023433

Printed in China
First printing, 2000
1 2 3 4 5 6 7 8 9 10 — 04 03 02 01 00

Contents

Introduction

The heat of the day's sun is waning as we take our after-dinner stroll, the traditional *passeggiata* that fills the streets with families chatting and nodding hellos as they pass. Facing the bustle of this joyful street scene, a sparkling glass case beckons. A hand-printed sign, *Nostra Produzione* (Our Production), dangles over the pastel rainbow of stainless-steel tubs filled with freshly made gelato, promising that the gelato is made on the premises. Another, smaller sign, *Produzione Artigianale* (Artisan Production), is taped inside the window. Our *passeggiata* is interrupted by the pleasure of selecting two or three flavors of this handcrafted gelato to fill a little paper cup. *"Leccalo dalle parti, se no ti sporchi"* ("Lick around the sides so it won't drip"), I hear a mother instructing a toddler with a creamy chocolate-filled cone.

Eating gelato, like drinking espresso, is a favorite Italian pastime. It is an opportunity to linger for conversation and people-watching, and a way to cool down from summer's unrelenting heat. In the south, gelato is even eaten for breakfast, served in a fresh brioche with a steaming cup of rich, black coffee!

History

Who invented frozen desserts? The Bible tells us that Isaac offered Abraham goat milk mixed with snow. The Chinese recorded eating a refreshing iced mixture as early as 200 B.C. From there, the process of making frozen sweets probably found its way to India and then Persia, and was brought to Sicily by the Arabs. In early Rome of A.D. 1, Emperor Nero Claudius Caesar was said to have had his slaves bring him snow and ice to be flavored with honey and fruits. In the seventh century, something known as *sharbet*, a crushed ice drink flavored with local fruit, was found among the Arab population of Sicily. The Greeks and the Turks made a lemon ice called by a similar name, *serbet* or *sharbat*, which literally means "fresh beverage." Other sources report that Marco Polo returned to Italy with a recipe for sherbet from the Far East in the twelfth century.

In the ruins of the taverns of Pompeii, a device was found that was equipped with what may have been a cooling unit containing a residue of lemon, wild berries, and fish gelatin.

7

Ice vendors collected blocks of ice and conserved them in salt in large caverns, then distributed them to upper-class taverns and wealthy families. A scoop of crushed ice was served with a drizzle of *saba* or *sapa*, a sweet syrup of reduced grape must. The beverage was drunk, then the flavored ice was eaten. It must have been a true luxury in the intense heat of a Campania summer.

Caterina de' Medici, who was born in Florence and was queen to Henry II in France in the mid-1500s, brought sorbetto to France. A few years earlier, the court of the Medici in Florence had held a contest to discover a "singular plate that has never been seen." Giuseppe Ruggeri, a vendor of chicken, showed up and prepared an exquisite sorbetto, and became quite famous as a result. When Caterina married Henry II, she brought Ruggeri with her to challenge the French chefs. He created splendid concoctions for the many heads of Europe. All of the powerful noble families wanted to know his secrets, but Caterina refused every request. Ruggeri, hated by all the cooks of the capital, was often physically accosted. Eventually, he left the recipe in an envelope for Caterina, having written on the back: "With your permission I return to my chickens, hoping that they won't remind me of the pleasures of my gelato."

In this same era, Florentine court architect and artist Bernardo Buontalenti was credited with inventing the first gelato to be churned over salt and ice. He built an ice cave in the Boboli Palace, and served his "marvels of *gelati*" at the Medici's many sumptuous banquets. Buontalenti invented a way to blend sweetened milk with a zabaglione of Malavasia wine and egg yolks and then freeze it. A gelato flavor is still named after him today: Buontalenti, a rich, eggy gelato with a warm yellow color due to the golden yolks of corn-fed chickens.

Gelato was not only a food for the nobles. By the early 1600s, every public square in Italy hosted a little three-wheeled cart of carved and painted wood selling *sorbetti*. Meanwhile, in the streets, other rolling vendors made the rounds to the sound of a little bell. In the heat of the summer, refreshing ices could be found at folk festivals and became a popular treat following religious gatherings.

Gelato found commercial success in France in 1686, where it was created by Sicilian Francesco Procopio dei Coltelli at the Café Procope in Paris. Procopio was a young man full of talent and enthusiasm. His grandfather, Francesco, a fisherman, had tried to invent a little machine for the preparation of sorbetto, but he had not succeeded in making it work. The young Francesco, tired of the fishing life, decided to see if he could find the secret. After many tries, he discovered the two principles for its success: using sugar in place of the honey, and adding salt to the ice to make it last longer. With the "fever of the gelato," he headed up to Paris and opened a shop near the Comédie-Française, whose noble and scholarly patrons embraced his offerings of iced fruits and almond milk sorbets.

Meanwhile, gelato found its way to England in 1650, in the court of King Charles I, whose pastry chef was Italian. Another Italian, Alessandro Tortoni, became famous in Paris at his Café Napolitain at the end of the eighteenth century, creating a frozen dessert that bears his name. Without a doubt, whether they invented it or not, Italians were the emissaries of the gelato gospel.

In Naples during the reign of the Bourbons, Duke Ippolito Cavalcanti di Bonvicino, as a hobby, wrote the *Trattato di cucina teorico-practica* (*The Theory and Practice of the Kitchen*), dedicating an entire chapter to the art of making *sorbetti*. One of the recipes was for a chocolate sorbetto made with sugar syrup, using snow. He also described "*gelati al forno*," created by a Bari pastry cook, Felice Lippolis: two slices of *pan di Spagna* made into a sandwich stuffed with gelato. Another, more comprehensive description for making fruit *gelati* was included in *Il Re dei cuochi*, an Italian cookbook published in 1885: "Fill a bucket with crushed ice and salt, set a second metal bucket with the ingredients in it, and churn the ingredients vigorously for about an hour, or until the mixture is creamy and smooth."

In the eighteenth and nineteenth centuries, it was believed that sorbets had beneficial digestive properties. The tradition of serving sorbet between heavy courses, still occasionally seen in fine dining establishments, was initiated. Today, some modern cookbooks include recipes for "digestive" *sorbetti*, flavored with basil, sage, celery, tomato, and even lettuce.

The word *gelato* is the past participle of the Italian verb *gelare*, to freeze. The term is often used in Italy for any frozen dessert, whether milk or water-based. In the most common definition, *gelati* are made from milk-based mixtures and *sorbetti* and *granite* are fruit-based. Sorbetto, called sorbet in French, is made from juice or strained fruit purée, whereas *cremolata* is made with unstrained puréed fruit. Granita is fruit-flavored icy granules, coarser than sorbetto, so slushy that in hot weather it is best served in a glass. Ideally, *gelati*, *sorbetti*, and *granite* should be made daily in small batches with no added chemical preservatives, emulsifiers, or stabilizers.

lower in fat, often with no more than 6 to 7 percent butterfat, gelato has much more flavor than American ice cream. This is because fat tends to coat the mouth, blocking the experience of the fresh and natural flavor. In addition, the best *gelaterie* use full-flavored seasonal products, maximizing the essence of the main ingredient. Another reason for the intense flavors is that gelato is kept at a warmer freezing temperature. The consistency is dense and velvety, with less air beaten into it. The softer texture glides through the mouth, and because it is not so cold, the taste buds do not become numb with freezing, but are open to accept more of the flavor.

Gelato, sorbetto, and granita flavors run the gamut from seasonal fresh fruits to popular essences including coffee and chocolate or liqueurs such as vin santo, Marsala, limoncello, or even grappa. Each bite packs a wallop of sensory stimulation, a celebration of the primary ingredient undisguised by additives or cloying, heavy ingredients that mask the original flavor. Though

As with most foods in Italy, each region has a local interpretation, whether in style or in the use of local ingredients. In the south, particularly in Sicily, gelato made with milk or fresh cheese may be thickened with a vegetable starch rather than with eggs. In central Italy, the base is a custard made with milk and eggs. In the north, the custard is richer, made by adding cream.

Your first decision on entering a *gelateria* is how much gelato you want to eat. In most *gelaterie* you pay first, then take your receipt to the counter to request your choice of flavors. Most often gelato is served from a little cup, usually paper, and eaten with a tiny, flat spade-shaped plastic spoon. Often, a display on the countertop shows the prices on samples. The smallest usually start at 1,500 to 2,000 lire, about a dollar. The size of the cup determines the number of flavors you can choose, and don't be surprised if the *gelataio* (the gelato maker) recommends complementary flavors. You can also request an *assaggio*, a taste, before making your final decision.

Most *gelaterie* also offer cones, though you may see the Italians eat the gelato first with a spoon, then consume the cone.

A number of desserts have been developed using *gelati* or *sorbetti*. The general classification of chilled or partially frozen desserts is *semifreddo*, which means "partly cold." It describes desserts made from a gelato base with whipped cream folded in, a technique that prevents the dessert from freezing completely. Also included in this category are mousses and molded desserts. *Cassate* and *bombe* are popular desserts of two or more flavors of gelato frozen in a domed, flat, round, or heart-shaped pan. Individual molds or frozen slices are called *pezzi duri*. Another prevalent dessert is a variety of gelato cake called *torta gelato*, made with gelato layered with sponge cake, meringue, candied fruit, cookie crumbs, and/or ladyfingers. Many of these desserts, such as a panettone filled with gelato, a favorite holiday sweet, are made at home with purchased *gelati*. The name for spumoni comes from *spuma*, which means foam. It is a light dessert, usually an egg-based gelato filled with semifreddo. *Zuccotto* is made in a similar way, with the addition of a layer of *pan di Spagna*, or sponge cake, which is often soaked with liqueur. The Sicilian *cassata* has even more layers, including *pan di Spagna*, and is covered with marzipan.

Gelateria/bar establishments offer dramatic presentations such as combinations of gelato with syrups, sauces, and whipped cream. One of my favorites is *affogato*, which literally means "drowned," a scoop of gelato served in a tall glass and topped with brandy, grappa, or hot coffee. In the summer it is pleasant to sip on a *frappé*, a blended drink made with gelato and fruit or espresso. Sometimes it is just a simple *macedonia* (fresh-fruit salad), topped with a scoop of gelato and *panna montata* (whipped cream). In the winter, some *gelaterie* offer *gelato caldo*, literally "warm gelato," a mousse or semifreddo of seasonal fruits, such as persimmons, or chestnuts.

A Tour of Gelaterie

Since gelato is said to have ancient origins in Sicily, we should start our tour of Italian *gelaterie* there.

Sicily's colorful and flavorful cuisine was created from its sun-drenched local foods and the delicacies imported from the countries of its many invaders over the centuries. Spices and plants with origins in faraway lands have found their way to the fertile soil of this island, and the foods and culture of the Moors, Greeks, Romans, Spanish, Bourbons, and the French are part of Sicilian cooking.

It is widely believed that sorbetto was adopted in the two hundred years of Saracen domination. The Arabs' "sophisticated and luxurious habits," along with their importation of sugar-cane, citrus, and almonds, led to the development of elaborate desserts. The moderate climate and the year-round availability of fruits made the island a perfect place to make sorbet, an art the Arabs apparently learned from the Chinese. Because they believed that sugar was healthful and had divine properties, sweet foods such as sorbetto were used in religious celebrations, a tradition that continues today in many of the convents and on annual feast days.

Today, Sicily grows 90 percent of the citrus for the Italian market. The fertile land surrounding Mt. Etna provides many of the natural ingredients that form the base of their magnificent *gelati*, such as cherries from Macchia and pistachios from Bronte, as well as honey, Avola almonds, walnuts, chestnuts, and wild strawberries. They have perfected liqueurs of lemon, mandarin, Rosolio (made from flower petals and spices), laurel leaves, and orange blossoms. Nearby Catania is famous for *cassata gelata*, bricks of vanilla or hazelnut gelato with a center of candied fruit and liqueur.

Just south, near Siracusa, is the honey-colored town of Noto. Noto was leveled in 1693 by a terrible earthquake, and completely rebuilt of ornate stone in the baroque style. Among the many folkloric celebrations held there, one of the most charming and colorful is the Primavera Barocca, a baroque salute to spring. The Infiorata di Via Nicolaci, held on the third Sunday of May, is a series of mosaics made of flower petals that carpet the length of the street. Some of these aromatic flowers also end up in the *sorbetti* and *gelati* of **Corrado Costanza**, a well-known pastry and gelato maker with almost fifty years' experience. I first read about him in Nick Malgieri's book, *Great Italian Desserts* (Little, Brown, 1990). I found reference to him again in *Il Buon Paese*, Slow Food's guide to Italian food experts, and again in Fred Plotkin's *Italy for the Gourmet Traveler* (Little,

Brown, 1997). Costanza's specialties continue to draw "foodies," but what captured me were the aromatic *sorbetti* and *gelati* made from the blossoms of roses and jasmine flowers. His tangerine sorbetto is the ultimate refreshing flavor on a steamy hot Sicilian day, bringing out the sweet essence of the local fruit. Also, Costanza makes a traditional granita from almond milk, thought to be one of the earliest types of ice made. It is made from local almonds, which are finely chopped and left to steep in water. The water is strained to yield a intensely flavorful almond milk, which is then sweetened and frozen to a granita.

Sicily is a food-lover's paradise, made both challenging and charming by the lack of tourism. Nibbling around the island by way of the coast, I found myself in Mondello, a beachy suburb of Palermo. In the early morning heat, I partook in a Sicilian breakfast tradition at **Antico Chiosco**, a *gelateria* and bar that serves a fresh brioche, a *cornetto*, filled with your choice of sorbetto. I chose raspberry.

Palermo was the Saracen capital of Sicily in 831 and remains the capital of the island today. It is a busy port, with all of the bustle of a major city's commerce, and reflects the diversity of its history. Food is celebrated with elaborate dishes created from the abundant supply of local and international ingredients. A visit to the colorful Arab-style shopping streets of Ballarò or Via della Vuccirìa reveals a rich source of local fresh and prepared products, as well as those from North Africa, the Mediterranean, and other parts of Europe. At night, when shopkeepers illuminate their wares with fantastically bright lights, all of your senses are bombarded.

In the heart of the city is **Gelateria Stancampiano**. In the tradition of his father before him, Umberto Stancampiano founded the business in the current location in 1974 and now runs it with the help of his brother, Giovanni, and their children. In fact, the whole family works in the food business; other brothers run the nearby *pasticceria* and bar a half-block away. In the gelato kiosk, just across from one of Palermo's busy train stations, I found the best pistachio gelato I have ever tasted. Among the forty flavors, I spotted the drab green tub immediately; it tasted like a creamy mouthful of aromatic pistachios. Much to my surprise, right next to it was another tub with the same label, a mound of fluorescent green gelato. When I asked the brothers Stancampiano which one they sold the most of, one told me the natural version sold more. He explained, "We make the real pistachio one for the adults; the brightly colored one is for the *bimbi*," the little children, who are attracted to its neon glow. The natural pistachio is made of fresh pistachios, from Bronte in western Sicily. It is made by creaming the nuts in a centrifuge at 45,000 spins per minute. As they become a paste, the sugar and the milk are added. The mixture is then pasteurized, cooled, and put in the machine to churn.

The second brother responded differently to my question; his impression was that they sold more of the brightly colored gelato. "It is made with a typical regional base called *pasta reale*, which is made of marzipan and artificial color. Because of the sugar in the *pasta reale*, it is sweeter and tastes more of almonds than pistachios," but, as he explained, "The people love it because *pasta reale* is the ingredient used to make the molded fruits and figures which are so popular here. It's a typical taste of Sicily, to which they are accustomed."

The *gelateria* is open almost year-round, closing only from mid-December to mid-January, and sometimes it doesn't close at all. The "regular" business hours are from 9 A.M. to 4 A.M., when the brothers cater to all kinds of customers, from teenagers who spend their afternoons sitting on their *motorini* parked in front of the shop, to small children buying tiny cones that have been dipped in chocolate and frozen. Sunday is a popular day to pick up a *torta gelato*, one of their molded desserts. In the winter, the crowds still gather for the *gelato caldo: semifreddi* and gelato mousses.

How is gelato made? There is great variation in the answer to this question. Some *gelaterie* buy the gelato already made and delivered in plastic tubs that fit right into the display unit. It is even possible to call the gelato *artigianale*, or artisan, by using a premade mix that is poured into a machine to be churned on site. But in order to have a natural product, made from fresh fruit without the stabilizers and emulsifiers needed for the instant kinds of *gelati*, much more time and labor are necessary.

I learned about this when I spent a half day with Antonio Lisciandro. Lisciandro's family came from Sicily. His father and grandfather were gelato makers; his family has been in the business for eighty-eight years. Antonio started working with them when he was fifteen. He and his wife, Loredana, have run the inspired **Gelateria Carabe** in Florence on via Ricasoli, near the Accademia, for ten years, and he has just opened a new *gelateria* in Vittoria Apuana, a suburb of Forte dei Marmi on the Tuscan coast. With an impressive backdrop of marble, Vittoria Apuana is a summer retreat with abundant markets, lush green summer growth, hotels with private beaches, and a *gelateria* every few meters.

"My art is the transformation of the *materie prime*, the main ingredients, which must be of the highest quality," Antonio explains, "A good example is the conversion of a tree to a table. The quality of the table will only be as good as the quality of the wood and the craftsmanship used to make it. Gelato is a living product; it evolves. My goal is how I can make the best possible *gelati*."

Handmade gelato is lower in fat than its commercial counterpart. *Industriale*, as the Italians call a nonartisan product, needs more fat and stabilizers to maintain the molecular structure and antioxidants to maintain color. Gelato is made by two actions, chilling and stirring. The purpose of the stirring is to add air, but not too much. Antonio's gelato has a maximum of 30 percent air, and usually 20 to 25 percent, depending on the gelato. *Industriale* is 60 percent air, much of which is artificially blown in to increase the volume.

For the most part, Antonio makes his *gelati*, *sorbetti*, and *granite* with only fruit, sugar, and water or milk. In some cases he uses carruba, a natural stabilizer made of carob bean gum. In low-fat mixtures, it prevents the formation of ice crystals by absorbing some of the extra water.

The *gelati* are kept at the lowest possible temperature to maintain their structure while not freezing them too hard. *Gelati* with more fat need colder temperatures, up to −10°C (the freezing temperature for milk mixtures) to −14°C. *Industriale gelati*, with their high fat content, need to be kept colder, down to −22°C. Antonio says, "In the summer, my customers prefer flavors with low-fat and low-sugar content; it takes three times longer to digest high-fat *gelati*. And, the flavor is better; it cleans and refreshes the mouth. Milk-based *gelati* make you feel that you need to have a drink of water."

In accordance with Italian sanitation laws, Antonio pasteurizes the milk and egg mixtures at 90°C for 4 minutes, then cools them to 4°C for 25 minutes. When I asked him if he was discouraged about the loss of flavor caused by using such high heat, he responded, "It is a necessary process; it pasteurizes the ingredients and kills the bacteria."

Antonio's secret for excellent *gelati* is "excellent ingredients. My lemons, pistachios, and *fichi d'India* [cactus pears] come from Sicily. You can't use a recipe, because every fruit is different every day—sometimes they are very ripe and don't need as much sugar, sometimes they do."

Even though Antonio lives in Tuscany, his style is very much reminiscent of his Sicilian roots. I went to Guido Ballerini to experience a historical Tuscan perspective. His family's *gelateria*, **Il Fantino**, goes back four generations in Campi Bisenzio, a suburb of Florence. Great grandfather Giuseppe, known as Il Fantino (the jockey), due to his short stature, delivered *gelati* on his bicycle. Guido's grandfather, also named Guido, followed in his footsteps, making the rounds

with a little cart pulled with a bicycle. His son, Giancarlo, modernized the business and used a Lambretta scooter.

Today, Giancarlo's three sons, Guido, Claudio, Marco, and his daughter, Carla, run a small store in this business suburb. Carla says, "I've worked here for thirty-four years, since I was

ten. I like people." And it's a good thing, for the line spills out the door, especially on Sundays when customers buy their gelato by the kilo. Guido keeps one machine next to the display counter running almost constantly to replenish directly to the stainless-steel tubs. He explains, "We make ten to twelve flavors at the most. I have to start at six in the morning, and we're usually not done until midnight. At the end of the day there is nothing left; we start completely fresh in the morning."

Guido's grandfather and great-grandfather offered fewer flavors, but the quality of ingredients was always the most important thing, a philosophy that has endured in each generation. The base they used is now called *crema vecchia maniera*, old-style *crema*, or custard. Sugar and egg yolks were beaten and added to hot milk and cream, then churned. In the past, the only flavoring used was vanilla, or

Cialde, or cones, can
be traced back to European
cookie makers in the
fifteenth century, specifically
the Viennese waffeln, or
wafers which were cooked
on special irons.

One of Italy's most
popular cialde companies
is Babbi. Gianluigi Babbi
carries on the family
tradition begun in 1953 in
Romagna. The company
also makes cookie wafers
of all shapes and sizes,
some filled with vanilla or
chocolate, others dipped
in chocolate.

sometimes Marsala. Today, Guido might add ground coffee, lemon zest, or maybe cinnamon. His modern-day base utilizes the same ingredients; the only difference is in the pasteurization, a hotter and lengthier exposure to high temperatures.

A visit to Florence isn't complete without a stop at **Vivoli**, renowned *gelateria* since 1930. Piero Vivoli and his daughter Silvana preside over an immaculate and enormous *laboratorio*, or workshop, while mother Simonetta and sister Patrizia work the counter. In spite of the amazing volume of gelato produced, Vivoli remains committed to using fresh and wholesome ingredients.

In addition to numerous *gelati* and *sorbetti* served by the cup (no cones used here), they also are masters of *torte*, gelato cakes. One of their specialties is zuccotto, a typical Tuscan dessert. Piero gave me a lesson in putting one together. First, he assembled all of the necessary ingredients: pan di Spagna, or homemade sponge cake, and cream whipped with sugar,

along with chopped chocolate and candied orange peel.

Piero sliced the pan di Spagna into 1/4-inch-thick slices and lined a smooth-sided mold with them, filling in any open spaces with custom-cut wedges. He then soaked the cake with liqueur. He spooned in the whipped cream and sprinkled it with a layer of chocolate. This was topped with a layer of pan di Spagna that was soaked again, and another layer of whipped cream sprinkled with the candied orange peel. This layering is continued until the dish is full, with one last layer of pan di Spagna to cover. Placed in the freezer for at least two hours, the zuccotto never completely freezes, due to the alcohol in the cake and the high fat content of the whipped cream. But it chills firmly enough that it can be sliced when unmolded (see recipe, page 94).

In Cuneo, in southern Piedmont, cheerful Claudio Elli began studying the art of gelato and pastry in the 1950s. In 1969, he moved with his wife, Maria Antonetta Boglione, a legal secretary, to Alessandria to open **Cremeria del Corso**. He started with a small bar-*gelateria-pasticceria*, offering only a few high-quality items in each section, along with the best coffee. He was an immediate success, and soon his wife came to work with him. The great flood of 1994 damaged his workshop, so the next year they decided to completely renovate and to expand to a grand cafe with two floors and 150 seats. Claudio's two sons, Enrico and Giampiero, came to work with him.

In the summer, cafe tables set under umbrellas invite passersby to pause in their *passeggiata* on the cobbled pedestrian-only Corso Roma to enjoy "*gelato viene prodotto giornalmente solo con materie prime naturali: uova, latte, panna, zucchero e frutta di stagione*": "gelato made daily only with the best-quality natural ingredients: eggs, milk, cream, sugar, and seasonal fruit."

One look at the kitchen, Enrico's domain, tells the whole story. Everything sparkles, from the gelato-making units to the pristine stainless-steel counters and shelves. On the shelves

are jars of freshly preserved fruit purées and nut pastes. Claudio pulls me aside and points around the kitchen: "*Pulita, pulita, pulita. . .*" His passion for cleanliness and purity is evident as I watch him wash strawberries three times, using a little bicarbonate of soda to disinfect them.

Enrico explains, "We use only fresh seasonal and local products, without the addition of any type of semi-industrial or industrial product, or something not made by nature." He has researched the best source for each of his ingredients, using, for example, milk from Milan, even though local milk would cost less. Though he can buy prepasteurized whole eggs and egg whites, he prefers to use fresh.

Claudio, smiling as always, interjects, "The gelato should be soft like butter," yet they churn it for only fifteen minutes for about 15 percent air volume. How do they get that consistency without stabilizers? Because the gelato is made daily, and doesn't need to be as stable as gelato that is held for several days or longer. They also use a cooked meringue

that is folded in, giving the *gelati* and *sorbetti* a silky consistency and body. As Enrico prepared a batch of *nocciola*, or hazelnut, gelato, I began to understand his commitment to quality. It starts with the kind of hazelnut, *tonda delle Langhe*, a local variety determined by professional chefs to have the best flavor and aroma for pastry and gelato. Even though it is local, it still costs more than hazelnuts from Turkey, Sicily, or Campania. "But," Enrico says, "because the flavor is so intense, you use less," and he pulls down a jar of paste that he has ground himself.

The parlor menu lists a variety of gelato compositions: *castagne di bosco*, made with marron glacé or chocolate gelato and whipped cream, and topped with candied chestnuts and hot chocolate sauce; *gianduiotto* features the superb local hazelnuts in a classic combination of mounds of hazelnut and chocolate gelato, garnished with hazelnut praline and caramel sauce. Enrico's playful side is displayed in the whimsical "spaghetti," *crema* gelato pressed through a

potato ricer to make a mound of spaghetti-like threads that is "sauced" with a fresh strawberry "ragu" and topped with crumbled amaretti that look like pieces of grated cheese.

Gelateria Stancampiano, Carabe, Il Fantino, and Cremeria del Corso are examples of artisan producers who take their work seriously. At the other end of the artisanal spectrum lie the industrial producers who make the gelato available in supermarkets or in freezer cases in many bars. Multinational businesses such as Unilever and Nestlé own Italian divisions that make popular stick ice creams. There is no denying the popularity of these products, which sell for only 800 lire (about 35 cents).

There does exist an industrial producer, however, who maintains all of the integrity of a one-man *gelateria*. Along the Tuscan coast to the south, in Castiglioncello, **Dai Dai** is a small-scale gelato company specializing in chocolate-coated gelato desserts. Antonio Bartoletti is best known for *Cassatina Dai Dai*,

An artisanal producer
is easily recognized by the
equipment in his or her
kitchen. Industrial gelato
requires only one machine:
The premixed base mixture
is poured in, and gelato
comes out. The artisan
requires separate machines
to control each step of
the process: pasteurization
of the natural raw ingre-
dients, homogenization,
and freezing.

*At Dai Dai, all of
the work is done by hand,
from the toasting of the
pine nuts to the whipping
of the cream and most
importantly, the cutting
of the gelato bricks and
hand-dipping them in
chocolate. The bricks are
then packaged by hand,
in printed brown wrappers,
and placed one by one into
boxes of pure cellulose.*

a brick of gelato with pine nuts, coffee, chocolate, or plain cream, covered in chocolate, and *bocconcini*, bite-sized chocolate-coated gelato cubes. He also produces *pezzi duri*, slices of fruit and cream *sorbetti*.

The name Dai Dai, which means "give it to me," originated from a man named Signore Tancredi who, in 1920, sold gelato from a little cart pulled by a mule in Castiglioncello. Antonio started his business in 1984, and for the first five years he personally made deliveries in his little Fiorino, sometimes driving all the way to Milan with only two boxes. When the business began to take off, he calculates he drove 150,000 kilometers (90,000 miles) in a year.

Antonio walked me through the process of making *Cassatina Dai Dai*. Three women (he calls them his *bambine*; most have worked with him for at least ten years) produce 200 kilograms (440 pounds) of the bricks per day, in small batches. They work quickly, and all of the work is done completely by hand, from the toasting of the pine nuts to the whipping of the cream, and most importantly, the cutting of the bricks and dipping them by hand in chocolate. The bricks are even packaged by hand in printed brown wrappers; the blocks are then placed one at a time into boxes made of pure cellulose.

The ingredients are the best available, such as milk from Piedmont, Pernigotti chocolate, and pine nuts from Pisa grown by a family who have been in that business for four generations. Other ingredients listed on the packaging are "fresh cream and fresh milk from the dairy, egg yolk quality A, sugar, wheat flour." One stabilizer, gelatin, is used.

All of these artisinal gelato makers described here make their products in volume using large equipment, but the methods are the same as what we will do at home: selection of high-quality ingredients, pasteurization (heating raw dairy and eggs to the proper temperature), homogenization (mixing), chilling, and churning.

Making Gelato at Home

Making your own gelato may be even better than buying it. Because the batch will be small, with very little air churned in, the result will be creamy and delicious. Because you will probably eat it the day it is made, the gelato will be fresh, and will not need stabilizers. The best results occur with the best ingredients. Seasonal ripe fruit is essential. Even the water is important: Use spring water, filtered, or bottled water, especially in areas where the tap water has been heavily treated.

As Leonardo da Vinci said, "*Quelli che si innamorano di sola pratica senza scienza so come l'nocchier che entra un navilio senza timon o bussola, che mai ha certezza dove si vada*": "Those enamored of practice without science are like the navigator who enters a boat without a compass and never knows with certainty where he is going." You can adjust gelato and sorbetto recipes somewhat, according to your personal taste and the maturity of the fruit, but there is a

science to the combination of ingredients and the techniques for freezing. For example, the more sugar or alcohol you use, the less the gelato or sorbetto will freeze. If you use too much of either, the mixture won't freeze at all. On the other hand, too little sugar will affect the texture, making it grainy. Texture can also be controlled by the temperature when freezing, especially when you use ice and salt. Cold, fast churning (using a lot of salt) yields a coarser dessert; using less salt and a longer churning time makes the gelato silkier.

Adding liqueur gives gelato a new flavor dimension. Grand Marnier and Cointreau are orange liqueurs, while Moscato has slightly less orange essence. Kirsch (cherry) and Chambord (raspberry) liqueurs both go well with pears or chocolate. For a hazelnut essence, try Frangelico. Some other, more rare, essences include Averna, a typical Sicilian favorite with a bitter coffee and chocolate taste, and Rosolio, made from rose petals, jasmine flowers, and orange blossoms, sometimes spiced with cinnamon

and cloves. Galliano is an old favorite made with herbs, berries, and spices, with tones of vanilla and anise.

Hard liquors can enhance iced desserts as well. Grappa spikes the taste of *sorbetti*; it is especially good with pear, currant, and raspberry. Rum and cognac warm up grape, peach, and apple *sorbetti* as well as some milk-based *gelati*. But remember: Too much alcohol will keep gelato or sorbetto from freezing completely. The higher the proof of the alcohol, the less you can use. See guidelines on page 106.

Because it has no stabilizers, homemade gelato doesn't keep in the freezer well; it becomes too hard. Better to make the base mixture ahead (up to three days) and keep it chilled until you are ready to churn. If the recipe calls for folding in whipped cream or beaten egg whites, wait until you're ready to churn before completing this step.

The first manual gelato-making machines came out at the end of nineteenth century, and the first successful electric version came out in 1929, created by Otello Cattabriga of Bologna, who is still producing commercial equipment for *gelaterie*.

Choosing the right gelato machine makes a difference; it is, as Antonio Lisciandro says, ". . . like the difference in a chicken that is roasted in an electric oven versus one that has been roasted in a gas oven or another cooked in a wood-burning oven."

Probably the easiest, least messy method is using one of the top-of-the-line machines with a built-in freezing unit. There is no ice and no salt to deal with. All you do is put the chilled mixture into the bowl, and in about thirty minutes you have fresh gelato. The bowls are easy to remove and clean. Three brands to look for are Il Gelataio Magnum, manufactured in Italy by Simac; Lussino, manufactured in Italy by Musso, a high-tech-looking unit with a stainless-steel external finish; and the Robot Coupe Piccolo.

But since gelato doesn't need tons of air churned into it, even the simplest ice cream maker will work. Several manual and electric units, such as Donvier, Krups, and Cuisinart, have metal liners which are prefrozen, also eliminating the need for ice and salt. The drawback is that you can only make one batch, as you will need to wait until the liner has time to freeze again.

White Mountain still makes old-fashioned wooden ice cream churns with a hand-crank as well as electric versions that maintain the tradition without the effort.

*Don't have an
ice cream machine?*

*Chill your gelato base
mixture well and place it
in a stainless steel bowl
in the freezer. When
partially frozen, beat the
mixture with a wire whisk
until it is creamy. Return
the bowl to the freezer
and repeat the process
again once or twice.*

Mascarpone Gelato

East of Florence, in the village of
San Francesco, Gelateria Sottani makes mascarpone
gelato with pine nuts. Here is my version.

2 cups whole milk

2 cups heavy cream

2/3 cup sugar

1 vanilla bean, split lengthwise

2 cups (16 ounces) mascarpone cheese at room temperature

1 teaspoon grated lemon zest

2/3 cup pine nuts, toasted (see page 106)

In a medium saucepan, combine the milk, cream, and sugar. Cook over medium heat, stirring until the sugar is dissolved, then cook until bubbles form around the edges of the pan. Remove from heat. Add the vanilla bean, scraping the seeds into the milk, and let stand for 30 minutes. Cover and refrigerate for at least 2 hours, or until thoroughly chilled.

Remove the vanilla pod. Stir in the mascarpone, lemon zest, and pine nuts. Transfer to an ice cream maker and freeze according to the manufacturer's instructions. *Makes 1 1/2 quarts; serves 6*

Vanilla Gelato

Vanilla, my daughter's favorite flavor,
is not very common in the Italian gelaterie. When
available, it is known as fior di latte.

1 1/2 cups heavy cream

1 1/2 cups whole milk

1 cup sugar

1/2 vanilla bean, split lengthwise

In a medium saucepan, combine the cream, milk, and sugar. Cook over medium heat, stirring until the sugar is dissolved, then cook until bubbles form around the edges of the pan. Remove from heat. Add the vanilla bean, scraping the seeds into the milk, and let stand for 30 minutes. Cover and refrigerate for at least 2 hours, or until thoroughly chilled.

Remove the vanilla pod and transfer the mixture to an ice cream maker. Freeze according to the manufacturer's instructions. *Makes 1 quart; serves 4*

Stracciatella

This is one of my favorite Italian ice creams.
The chocolate pieces are so fine they seem to have
been shaved or finely grated.

1¹/₂ cups heavy cream

1¹/₂ cups whole milk

1¹/₄ cups sugar

¹/₂ vanilla bean, split lengthwise

2 ounces semisweet chocolate, finely chopped

In a medium saucepan, combine the cream, milk, and sugar. Cook over medium heat, stirring until the sugar is dissolved, and then cook until bubbles form around the edges of the pan. Remove from heat. Add the vanilla bean, scraping the seeds into the milk, and let stand for 30 minutes. Cover and refrigerate for at least 2 hours, or until thoroughly chilled.

Remove the vanilla pod and stir in the chocolate pieces. Transfer to an ice cream maker and freeze according to the manufacturer's instructions. *Makes 1 quart; serves 4*

Chestnut Honey Gelato

The smoky flavor of chestnut honey is
intensely apparent in this rich gelato. For a lighter flavor,
substitute orange blossom or lavender honey.

2 cups whole milk

¹/₂ cup chestnut honey

1 cup heavy cream

In a medium saucepan, heat the milk over medium heat until bubbles form around the edges of the pan. Add the honey and stir until dissolved. Remove from heat and let cool. Refrigerate for at least 2 hours, or until thoroughly chilled.

In a deep bowl, beat the cream until soft peaks form. Fold the whipped cream into the milk mixture and transfer it to an ice cream maker. Freeze according to the manufacturer's instructions. *Makes 1 quart; serves 4*

Hazelnut Gelato

Nocciola, or hazelnut, is a classic Italian gelato flavor. The nuts are grown

in Turkey, Spain, Greece, the United States, and Italy. The preferred variety is tonda delle Langhe,

from Piedmont, full of fragrance and long-lasting flavor.

1/2 cup (4 ounces) hazelnuts, toasted, and skinned (see page 106)

2/3 cup sugar

3 cups whole milk

Pinch of salt

6 egg yolks

1/4 cup heavy cream

In a food processor, combine the hazelnuts with 1/3 cup of the sugar and grind until fine.

In a medium saucepan, combine the milk and salt. Add the ground hazelnuts and heat the mixture over medium heat until bubbles form around the edges of the pan. Remove from heat and cool. Cover and refrigerate overnight. Return to a saucepan and heat until bubbles form again.

In a blender or food processor, beat the remaining sugar and egg yolks together until very thick. With the machine running, gradually add the hot milk.

Return the mixture to the saucepan. Cook over medium heat, stirring constantly with a wooden spoon, for 6 to 8 minutes, until the mixture thickens slightly and coats the back of the spoon. Remove from heat and set the pan in a bowl of ice water. Stir for 2 minutes to cool the mixture. Stir in the cream. Cover and refrigerate for at least 2 hours, or until thoroughly chilled.

Transfer the mixture to an ice cream maker and freeze according to the manufacturer's instructions. *Makes 1 1/2 quarts; serves 6*

Chocolate-Hazelnut Gelato

Gianduia, Piedmont's heavenly combination of chocolate and hazelnuts, is eaten

as a candy, a sauce, or an absolutely divine gelato.

3¹/2 cups hazelnuts, toasted, and
skinned (see page 106)

4¹/2 cups whole milk

6 ounces semisweet chocolate, coarsely chopped

¹/2 cup sugar

5 egg yolks

Chocolate Cream Sauce (page 105) for topping

In a food processor, finely grind 3 cups of the hazelnuts; set aside. Coarsely chop the remaining ¹/2 cup hazelnuts and set aside.

In a medium saucepan, heat the milk over medium heat until bubbles form around the edges of the pan. Add the ground hazelnuts, remove from heat, and let stand for at least 45 minutes at room temperature, or up to overnight in the refrigerator.

Strain the milk through a fine-meshed sieve lined with dampened cheesecloth, pressing to extract as much milk as possible. Return the milk to the saucepan and add the chocolate. Simmer over low heat, stirring, until melted.

In a blender or food processor, beat the sugar and egg yolks together until very thick. With the machine running, gradually add the chocolate mixture. Return the mixture to the saucepan.

Cook over medium heat, stirring constantly with a wooden spoon, for 6 to 8 minutes, or until the custard thickens and coats the back of the spoon. Remove from heat and set the pan in a bowl of ice water. Stir for 2 minutes to cool the mixture. Cover and refrigerate for at least 2 hours, or until thoroughly chilled.

Transfer the mixture to an ice cream maker and freeze according to the manufacturer's instructions.

Top each serving with chocolate sauce and sprinkle with the coarsely chopped hazelnuts. *Makes 1¹/2 quarts; serves 6*

Chestnuts are the
harbinger of fall. In Italy,
cars are often pulled
off the side of the road so
families can gather
a basket of the fuzzy nuts.
On the streets in the
villages, vendors sell them
from carts, warm and
redolent with smoke.

Chestnut Gelato

*Fall is chestnut season. On the streets, vendors sell roasted chestnuts fresh from
the coals in little brown paper bags. When not in season, this gelato can also be made from canned purée;
just be careful to taste and adjust the sugar if you buy sweetened purée.*

2 cups whole milk

1/2 vanilla bean, split lengthwise

2/3 cup sugar

4 egg yolks

1 cup (8 ounces) unsweetened chestnut purée

1 cup heavy cream

In a medium saucepan, cook the milk over medium heat until bubbles form around the edges of the pan. Add the vanilla bean, scraping the seeds into the milk. Remove from heat and let stand for 30 minutes to infuse. Remove the pod and reheat the milk until bubbles form again. Cover to keep hot.

In a blender or food processor, beat the sugar and egg yolks together until very thick. Add the chestnut purée and process until blended. With the machine running, gradually add the hot milk. Return the mixture to the saucepan.

Cook over medium heat, stirring constantly with a wooden spoon, for 6 to 8 minutes, until the mixture thickens and coats the back of the spoon. Remove from heat and set the pan in a bowl of ice water. Stir for 2 minutes to cool the mixture. Stir in the cream. Cover and refrigerate for at least 2 hours, or until thoroughly chilled.

Transfer the mixture to an ice cream maker. Freeze according to the manufacturer's instructions. *Makes 1 1/2 quarts; serves 6*

Pistachio Gelato

Pistachio gelato is the benchmark by which many gelaterie are judged. You can tell at

a glance if an artificial base has been used, just by the color. If the gelato maker is using real pistachio nuts,

the color will be an almost drab green. If the bin flashes a neon green, keep walking!

1 cup (6 ounces) shelled pistachios
(about 12 ounces in the shell)

3 cups whole milk

3/4 cup sugar

In a food processor or coffee grinder, grind the pistachio to a fine powder, reserving a few whole ones for garnish.

In a medium saucepan, combine the milk and sugar. Cook over medium heat, stirring until the sugar is dissolved, and bubbles form around the edges of the pan. Remove from heat, add the pistachios, cool, cover, and refrigerate overnight.

Strain the milk mixture through a fine-meshed sieve, pressing on the nuts with the back of a large spoon to get as much liquid from the nuts as possible. Transfer to an ice cream maker and freeze according to the manufacturer's instructions. *Makes 1 quart; serves 4*

Grape Gelato with Saba

Saba (or sapa) has been known since ancient times. It is a syrup made from cooked and reduced grapes, the same process used in making traditional balsamic vinegar. Some producers of balsamic vinegar sell this unfermented cooked grape must to serve spooned over desserts (see Resources, page 108).

2 pounds sweet seedless red grapes

1 cup apple juice

3/4 cup sugar

3 cups whole milk

Pinch of salt

6 egg yolks

Saba for topping

In a medium saucepan, combine the grapes, apple juice, and 1/4 cup of the sugar. Cook over medium-low heat, stirring occasionally, for 25 to 30 minutes until the grapes are very tender and the mixture has thickened. Set aside to cool.

In a medium saucepan, combine the milk and salt. Cook over medium heat until bubbles form around the edges of the pan.

In a blender or food processor, beat the remaining 1/2 cup sugar and egg yolks together until very thick. With the machine running, gradually add the hot milk. Return the mixture to the saucepan.

Cook over medium heat, stirring constantly with a wooden spoon, for 6 to 8 minutes, or until the mixture thickens and coats the back of the spoon. Remove from heat and set the pan in a bowl of ice water. Stir for 2 minutes to cool the mixture. Cover and refrigerate for at least 2 hours, or until thoroughly chilled.

In a blender or food processor, combine the chilled custard and the cooked grapes and purée until smooth. Transfer to an ice cream maker and freeze according to the manufacturer's instructions.

Serve drizzled with *saba. Makes 11/2 quarts; serves 6*

Banana Gelato

If gelato can be "comfort food," this is it. You might need to adjust the sugar if you use very ripe bananas.

Try to avoid touching the flesh of the bananas while peeling them to keep them from browning.

4 1/2 cups whole milk

4 ripe bananas, peeled and chopped

Juice of 1 lemon

1/2 cup sugar

5 egg yolks

In a medium saucepan, heat the milk over medium heat until bubbles form around the edges of the pan. Set aside and cover to keep hot.

In a blender or food processor, purée the bananas, lemon juice and 1/4 cup of the sugar until smooth. Set aside.

In the blender or food processor, beat the remaining 1/4 cup sugar and the egg yolks together until very thick. With the machine running, gradually add the hot milk. Return the mixture to the saucepan.

Cook over medium heat, stirring constantly with a wooden spoon for 6 to 8 minutes, or until the mixture thickens and coats the back of the spoon. Remove from heat and set the pan in a bowl of ice water. Stir for 2 minutes to cool the mixture. Stir in the banana mixture. Cover and refrigerate for at least 2 hours, or until thoroughly chilled.

Transfer the mixture to an ice cream maker and freeze according to the manufacturer's instructions. *Makes 1 1/2 quarts; serves 6*

Persimmon Gelato

Persimmons are available only in the fall.
Creamy persimmon gelato makes a delicious partner
for pumpkin pie at the holidays.

1 cup sugar

1 cup spring water

2 fresh Fuyu persimmons
(about 12 ounces total), peeled

1 cup heavy cream

In a medium saucepan, combine the sugar and water. Cook over medium heat, stirring until the sugar has dissolved. Set aside to cool.

In a blender or food processor, purée the persimmons. Blend in the cooled sugar syrup and transfer to a large bowl. Refrigerate for at least 2 hours, or until thoroughly chilled.

In a deep bowl, beat the cream until soft peaks form. Fold it into the persimmon mixture and transfer it to an ice cream maker. Freeze according to the manufacturer's instructions. *Makes 1 quart; serves 4*

Peach Gelato

It is easy to peel peaches (see Techniques, page 106).
You can also try substituting nectarines or apricots in this
recipe when they are ripe and in season.

4 cups whole milk

4 ripe peaches, peeled, pitted, and
chopped (about 2 cups)

Juice of 1 lemon

3/4 cup sugar

4 egg yolks

Follow the same instructions for Banana Gelato (page 46), substituting puréed peaches for the bananas. In step 3, beat the remaining 1/2 cup sugar and the egg yolks together until very thick. Continue as directed. *Makes 1 1/2 quarts; serves 6*

Zabaglione Gelato with Figs

Marsala, a Sicilian fortified wine, is most commonly used to flavor zabaglione, a warm custardlike dessert often served over fresh fruit. Here, the custard is used as a base for gelato, which is served over fresh figs.

²/₃ cup sugar

6 egg yolks

¹/₄ cup sweet Marsala

2¹/₄ cups whole milk

²/₃ cup heavy cream

Pinch of salt

12 ripe fresh figs, stemmed and halved

In a blender or food processor, beat the sugar and egg yolks together until pale in color. With the machine running, pour in the Marsala. Transfer the mixture to a double boiler over simmering water and cook, whisking constantly, for 8 to 10 minutes, or until thickened.

In a medium saucepan, combine the milk, cream, and salt. Heat over medium heat until bubbles form around the edge of the pan. Gradually add the hot milk to the Marsala mixture, whisking constantly. Remove the pan from heat and place it in a bowl of cold water, stirring for at least 2 minutes to cool the mixture. Cover and refrigerate for at least 2 hours, or until thoroughly chilled.

Transfer the mixture to an ice cream maker and freeze according to the manufacturer's directions.

Arrange the figs on individual serving plates and spoon the gelato on top. *Makes 1¹/₂ quarts; serves 6*

Amaretto–Poached Pear Gelato

Serve this creamy pear gelato with a little glass of delicate but nutty amaretto liqueur.

2 cups pear or apple juice

1 cup amaretto di Saronno

1/2 cup plus 2/3 cup sugar

6 pears, peeled, halved, and cored

2/3 cup heavy cream

2 1/4 cups whole milk

Pinch of salt

6 egg yolks

1/2 cup hazelnuts, toasted, skinned, and chopped (see page 106)

In a large saucepan, combine the pear or apple juice, amaretto, and the 1/2 cup sugar. Heat the mixture over medium heat, stirring until the sugar is dissolved. Add the pears and poach for 35 to 40 minutes, or until tender but not falling apart. Using a slotted spoon, transfer the pears to a plate. Reduce the cooking liquid for 20 minutes, or until slightly thickened. Set aside to cool. Stir in the cream. Cover and refrigerate the pears and liquid separately until needed.

In a medium saucepan, combine the milk and salt. Heat over medium heat until bubbles form around the edges. Remove from heat and cover to keep hot.

In a blender or food processor, blend the 2/3 cup sugar and the egg yolks together until very thick and smooth. With the machine running, gradually add the hot milk.

Return the mixture to the saucepan. Cook over medium heat, stirring constantly with a wooden spoon, for 6 to 8 minutes, until the mixture thickens slightly and coats the back of the spoon. Remove the pan from heat and set it in a bowl of ice water. Stir for 2 minutes to cool the mixture. Cover and refrigerate for at least 2 hours, or until thoroughly chilled.

Chop 6 of the pear halves, refrigerate the remaining 6 for serving. In a blender or food processor, purée the chilled custard and the chopped pears until smooth. Freeze in an ice cream maker according to the manufacturer's instructions.

To serve, arrange a pear half on each plate. Reheat the reduced cooking liquid. Scoop gelato on top of each pear half, spoon some of the reduced cooking liquid over, and garnish with the chopped hazelnuts. *Makes 1 1/2 quarts; serves 6*

Caffè Latte Gelato

Hardcore coffee-lovers can intensify the flavor of this coffee gelato by doubling the amount of ground coffee.

It is essential to grind the coffee fresh and as fine as possible to extract the most flavor.

2 cups whole milk

1/2 cup coffee beans, freshly ground to
a very fine powder

2/3 cup sugar

5 egg yolks

1 cup heavy cream

Whipped cream and chocolate-covered
coffee beans for garnish

In a medium saucepan, combine the milk and ground coffee. Bring to a low simmer over very low heat and cook for 20 minutes. Cover and let stand for 30 minutes, or refrigerate overnight. Strain the milk through a fine-meshed strainer. In a medium saucepan, heat the milk over medium heat until bubbles form around the edges of the pan. Set aside and cover to keep hot.

In a blender or food processor, blend the sugar and egg yolks together until very thick and smooth. With the machine running, gradually add the hot milk.

Transfer the mixture to the saucepan and cook over medium heat, stirring constantly with a wooden spoon, for 6 to 8 minutes, until the mixture thickens slightly and coats the back of the spoon. Remove the pan from heat and set it in a bowl of ice water. Stir for 2 minutes to cool the mixture. Cover and refrigerate for at least 2 hours, or until thoroughly chilled.

In a deep bowl, beat the cream until soft peaks form. Fold the whipped cream into the custard mixture. Transfer to an ice cream maker and freeze according to the manufacturer's instructions.

Serve garnished with whipped cream and chocolate-covered coffee beans. *Makes 1 1/2 quarts; serves 6*

Custard Gelato

One of the most popular flavors in gelaterie in Italy is crema, a simple frozen custard unenhanced by any flavoring.

It has a rich yellow color due to the brightness of the yolks of Italian corn-fed chickens.

2¼ cups whole milk

Pinch of salt

2/3 cup sugar

6 egg yolks

2/3 cup heavy cream

In a medium saucepan, combine the milk and salt. Heat the milk over medium heat until bubbles form around the edges of the pan. Set aside and cover to keep hot.

In a blender or food processor, blend the sugar and egg yolks together until very thick and smooth. With the machine running, gradually add the hot milk. Return the mixture to the saucepan and cook over medium heat, stirring constantly with a wooden spoon, for 6 to 8 minutes, or until the mixture thickens slightly and coats the back of the spoon. Remove the pan from heat and set it in a bowl of ice water. Stir for 2 minutes to cool the mixture. Cover and refrigerate for 2 hours, or until thoroughly chilled.

In a deep bowl, beat the cream until soft peaks form. Fold the whipped cream into the custard mixture. Transfer to an ice cream maker and freeze according to the manufacturer's instructions. *Makes 1½ quarts; serves 6*

Florentine Rice Gelato

The best gelato di riso I tasted was from Gelateria Il Fantino in Campi Bisenzio, near Florence.

Since Guido Ballerini wouldn't part with his recipe, I tried to re-create it using a basic vanilla base. It is best

to use long-grain rice; it has less starch, so the grains don't stick together when cooking.

6½ cups whole milk

1 cup sugar

1 cup long-grain rice, rinsed well

⅔ cup heavy cream

Pinch of salt

1 vanilla bean, split lengthwise

6 egg yolks

½ teaspoon freshly grated nutmeg

In a large saucepan, heat 4 cups of the milk. Add ⅓ cup of the sugar and stir until the sugar is dissolved. Add the rice and simmer for 1 hour, stirring frequently and mixing any skin that forms back into the mixture. The rice will be very tender, and the mixture will have thickened. Set aside to cool, stirring occasionally to keep it from clumping. Stir in the cream. Cover and refrigerate for at least 2 hours, or until thoroughly chilled.

In a medium saucepan, combine the remaining 2½ cups milk, the salt, and vanilla bean, scraping the seeds from the pod into the milk. Cook over medium heat until bubbles form around the edges of the pan. Remove from heat and remove the vanilla pod. Cover to keep hot.

In a blender or food processor, beat the remaining ⅔ cup sugar and the egg yolks together until very thick. Gradually add the hot milk. Return the mixture to the saucepan.

Cook over medium heat, stirring constantly with a wooden spoon, for 6 to 8 minutes, or until the custard thickens and coats the back of the spoon. Remove from heat and set the pan in a bowl of ice water. Stir for 2 minutes to cool the mixture. Cover and refrigerate for at least 2 hours, or until thoroughly chilled.

Stir the rice and nutmeg into the custard. Transfer to an ice cream maker and freeze according to the manufacturer's instructions. *Makes 2 quarts; serves 8*

*Although rice originated
in Asia, Italy now produces
60 percent of the rice for the
European market. Originally
imported by the early
Romans for medicinal and
cosmetic purposes, this
grain has clearly reached
a high culinary stature.*

Sorbetti & Granite

Orange Sorbetto

This easy do-ahead dessert is charmingly presented in a hollowed-out orange shell.

Lemon Granite and Sorbetto (page 79) can be similarly served in lemon shells.

2 oranges

2 cups spring water

1/2 cup sugar

1 teaspoon grated orange zest

1 egg white

Cut the oranges in half and scoop the pulp with a spoon, taking care not to puncture the skin. Set the shells aside. Place the pulp in a blender or food processor and add the water, sugar, and orange zest. Blend until the sugar is dissolved.

Strain the pulp mixture through a fine-meshed sieve, pressing out as much liquid from the pulp as possible with the back of a large spoon. Discard the pulp. Refrigerate the mixture for at least 2 hours, or until thoroughly chilled.

Transfer to an ice cream maker and freeze according to the manufacturer's instructions until partially frozen. Add the egg white and continue to freeze until firm.

Scoop the sorbetto into the reserved orange shells and freeze until ready to serve. *Makes 1 quart; serves 4*

Cactus Pear Sorbetto

Found in kitchens the world over, fico d'India, literally Indian fig, is the fruit of the Opuntia cactus.
Antonio Lisciandro of Gelateria Carabe demonstrates how he turns this magically colored fruit into festive gelato
and sorbetto. This base mixture also makes a delicious drink, mixed with vodka or rum.

1 pound fresh cactus pears, peeled (see page 106)

1 cup spring water

1/2 cup sugar

In a blender or food processor, combine all the ingredients and process until smooth. Strain through a fine-meshed sieve. Refrigerate for at least 2 hours, or until thoroughly chilled.

Transfer the mixture to an ice cream maker and freeze according to the manufacturer's instructions. *Makes 1 quart; serves 4*

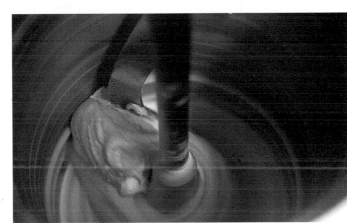

Melon Sorbetto

This shockingly simple sorbetto is unbelievably fresh tasting.
Try it also with watermelon or honeydew melon. Garnish with a slice
of fresh melon for an attractive presentation.

$^1/_2$ cantaloupe, peeled, seeded, and
chopped (about 2 cups)

1 cup spring water

$^1/_2$ cup sugar

Combine all the ingredients in a blender or food processor and
process until smooth. Refrigerate for at least 2 hours, or until
thoroughly chilled.

Transfer to an ice cream maker and freeze according to
the manufacturer's instructions. *Makes 1 quart; serves 4*

Strawberry Sorbetto

For a very silky sorbetto, strain the strawberries through

a fine-meshed sieve after puréeing.

$^1/_2$ cup sugar

$^1/_4$ cup spring water

4 cups fresh strawberries, hulled

1 egg white

In a medium saucepan, combine the sugar and water. Cook over medium heat, stirring until the sugar dissolves. Set aside to cool completely.

In a blender or food processor, purée the strawberries. You should have about 2 cups purée. Stir the purée into the cooled sugar syrup. Refrigerate for at least 2 hours until chilled.

Transfer to an ice cream maker and freeze according to the manufacturer's instructions until partially frozen. Add the egg white and continue to freeze until firm. *Makes 1$^1/_4$ quarts; serves 4*

Plum Sorbetto

*Create a leaning tower of plum with fresh plum slices
and rounds of plum sorbetto.*

I pound fresh plums, peeled,
seeded, pitted, and chopped (about 2 cups),
plus 6 whole plums for garnish

1 cup spring water

1/2 cup sugar

In a blender or food processor, combine all the ingredients and process until smooth. Refrigerate for at least 2 hours, or until thoroughly chilled. Transfer to an ice cream maker and freeze according to the manufacturer's instructions.

When firm, transfer to a 9-inch square baking dish. Smooth the top and place in the freezer for at least 1 hour.

To serve, slice the 6 reserved plums crosswise into 4 rounds each. Use a 2-inch biscuit cutter to cut the sorbetto into 18 rounds. Quickly stack 3 rounds of sorbetto between 4 slices of plum. Serve at once. *Makes 18 rounds; serves 6*

Kiwi Sorbetto

*If you prefer a silky green sorbetto, strain out
the little black seeds after puréeing.*

3/4 cup sugar

1/4 cup spring water

2 pounds ripe kiwis

2 tablespoons fresh lemon juice

1 egg white

In a medium saucepan, combine the sugar and water over medium heat, stirring, until the sugar dissolves. Set aside to cool.

Reserve 1 kiwi for garnish. Peel and chop the remaining kiwis. In a blender or food processor, combine the chopped kiwis and lemon juice; purée until smooth. Stir the purée into the cooled sugar syrup. Refrigerate for at least 2 hours until chilled.

Transfer the mixture to an ice cream maker and freeze according to the manufacturer's instructions until partially frozen. Add the egg white and continue to freeze until firm.

Peel and slice the reserved kiwi. Scoop the sorbetto into clear glass cups and top each with a slice of kiwi. *Makes 1 1/2 quarts; serves 6*

Blood Orange–Campari Sorbetto

Campari is a bitter apéritif with a glorious color similar to that of blood oranges. This sorbetto is also good made with grapefruits (increase the sugar to 1 1/2 cups).

10 blood oranges

1 cup sugar

1 egg white

1/4 cup Campari

Squeeze 9 of the oranges, reserving 1 orange for garnish. You should have about 3 cups juice. In a medium bowl, combine the orange juice and sugar and stir until the sugar is dissolved. Refrigerate for at least 2 hours until chilled.

Transfer the mixture to an ice cream maker and freeze according to the manufacturer's instructions until partially frozen. Add the egg white and continue to freeze until firm. Add the Campari and continue to freeze until firm again.

Peel the remaining orange and cut crosswise into 1/4-inch slices. Serve the sorbets garnished with the slices. *Makes 1 quart; serves 4*

Pear-Grappa Sorbetto

Grappa is a distilled alcohol made from the pressed grapes used for wine. Because the flavor of grappa is so intense, you will need only a small amount. It also combines well with strawberries, raspberries, and currants.

1 pound ripe pears, peeled, seeded, and chopped

1 cup spring water

1/2 cup sugar

2 tablespoons fresh lemon juice

1 egg white

2 tablespoons grappa

In a blender or food processor, combine the pears, water, sugar, and lemon juice. Process until smooth. Cover and refrigerate for at least 2 hours until chilled.

Transfer the mixture to an ice cream maker and freeze according to the manufacturer's instructions until partially frozen. Add the egg white and continue to freeze until firm. Add the grappa and continue to freeze until firm again. *Makes 1 quart; serves 4*

Raspberry Sorbetto

The raspberries macerated in Chambord can be used as a topping for other gelati and sorbetti as well.

3/4 cup sugar

1/2 cup spring water

4 cups fresh raspberries

Juice of 1/2 lemon

1 egg white

1/2 cup Chambord liqueur

In a medium saucepan, combine the sugar and water over medium heat, stirring, until the sugar dissolves. Set aside to cool.

In blender or food processor, purée 3 1/2 cups raspberries until smooth. Strain in a fine-meshed sieve to remove the seeds. Stir the purée into the cooled sugar syrup. Stir in the lemon juice. Refrigerate for at least 2 hours until chilled.

Transfer the mixture to ice cream maker and freeze according to the manufacturer's instructions until partially frozen. Add the egg white and continue to freeze until firm.

In a small bowl, combine remaining raspberries and the Chambord. Serve sorbetto with a spoonful of the raspberry mixture drizzled over the top of each serving. *Makes 1 quart; serves 4*

Blackberry-Sangiovese Sorbetto

Sangiovese is the grape used to make Chianti. A young fruity wine, it is an interesting complement to berry sorbetti.

3/4 cup sugar

1/2 cup spring water

4 cups fresh blackberries

1 egg white

1/2 cup Sangiovese wine

In a medium saucepan, combine the sugar and water; heat over medium heat, stirring, until the sugar dissolves. Set aside to cool.

In blender or food processor, purée the blackberries until smooth. Strain in a fine-meshed sieve to remove the seeds. Stir the purée into the cooled sugar syrup. Refrigerate for at least 2 hours until chilled.

Transfer the mixture to an ice cream maker and freeze according to the manufacturer's instructions until partially frozen. Add the egg white and continue to freeze until firm. Add the wine and continue to freeze until firm again. *Makes 1 quart; serves 4*

Sorbetto Bellini

The white peaches of the Veneto inspired a bartender at Harry's Bar in Venice to create

the Bellini cocktail, using the local Prosecco, a sparkling white wine, and a peach purée. In this variation,

the purée is made into sorbetto and served in glasses of the wine.

5 white peaches, peeled and pitted (see page 106)

1/4 cup fresh raspberries

2 cups spring water

2/3 cup sugar

2 bottles Prosecco or other sparkling white wine

In a blender or food processor, combine 4 of the peaches, raspberries, water, and sugar. Process until smooth. Transfer to an ice cream maker and freeze according to the manufacturer's instructions. Transfer to an airtight container and put in the freezer for 1 hour.

To serve, fill each of 12 champagne flutes two-thirds full with Prosecco or other sparkling wine. Slice the remaining peach into 12 thin slices. Using a melon baller, scoop 2 to 3 balls of the sorbetto into each glass, gently sliding them into the sparkling wine. Add a peach slice to the rim of each glass and serve at once. *Makes 1 1/2 quarts; serves 12*

Rose Petal Sorbetto

In Sicily, it is not uncommon to find sorbetti made from fragrant petals, such as jasmine or orange blossom.

If rose petals are unavailable, substitute 1 tablespoon bottled rose water.

1³/4 cups sugar

1¹/2 cups spring water

8 cups unsprayed aromatic fresh pink rose petals

Juice of 1 orange

Juice of ¹/2 lemon

2 egg whites

In a medium saucepan, combine the sugar and water and cook over medium-high heat, stirring until the sugar dissolves. Remove from the heat and add the rose petals. Let stand for 30 minutes. Refrigerate for at least 2 hours, or until thoroughly chilled.

Strain out and discard the rose petals. Add the orange and lemon juice to the syrup. Transfer the syrup to an ice cream maker and freeze according to the manufacturer's instructions until partially frozen. In a large bowl, beat the egg whites until soft peaks form. Stir into the sorbetto until blended. Continue to freeze until firm. *Makes 1 quart; serves 4*

Almond Granita

Almond milk has a surprisingly rich, yet delicate flavor that is maintained even when frozen.

In hot weather, it is very refreshing.

2 cups slivered almonds

2/3 cup sugar

4 cups spring water

In a food processor, grind the almonds to a fine paste. Add 1 cup of the water, and process with the almonds. Let stand for 1 hour. Strain through a fine-meshed sieve, stirring and pressing on the almond paste with the back of a large spoon to release as much liquid as possible. Set the almond milk aside. Return the almond paste to the food processor, and add 1 more cup water. Process, let stand, and strain as before. Repeat this process two more times. Reserve the almond milk and discard the almond paste.

In a medium bowl, combine the almond milk and sugar, stirring to dissolve the sugar. Pour into a 9-inch round or square baking dish. Freeze until the mixture becomes slushy around edges, about 30 minutes. Stir to break up the ice crystals. Continue freezing, stirring the mixture every 20 minutes, until it is slushy, about 1 hour. *Makes 1 quart; serves 4*

*On the southeastern coast
of Sicily, below Siracusa, is
the baroque village of Noto
where Corrado Costanza
has been making gelati for
fifty years. One of his
specialties, a granita made
from almond milk, uses the
renowned local almonds
from Avola.*

Lemon Granita

Lemon granita is one of the Italian classics, simple and refreshing. This recipe can also be used to make a sorbetto by freezing the mixture in an ice cream maker until partially frozen. Add an egg white and continue to process until firm. For an interesting presentation, serve in hollowed lemon halves, similar to the recipe for Orange Sorbetto (page 61).

2 cups spring water

1 cup sugar

1 cup fresh lemon juice

1 teaspoon grated lemon zest

In a large bowl, combine all the ingredients and stir until the sugar is dissolved.

Pour into a 9-inch round or square baking dish. Freeze until the mixture becomes slushy around the edges, about 30 minutes. Stir to break up the ice crystals. Continue freezing, stirring the mixture every 20 minutes, until it is slushy, about 1 hour. *Makes 1 quart; serves 4*

Coffee Granita

A Sicilian classic, coffee granita is wonderful served in a fresh brioche (page 90) for breakfast

on a hot day, or as an after-dinner refreshment in small elegant glasses.

4 cups hot, freshly brewed espresso or strong coffee

$^1/_2$ cup sugar

In a medium bowl, combine the espresso and sugar, stirring to dissolve the sugar. Set aside to cool. Pour into a 9-inch round or square baking dish. Freeze until the mixture becomes slushy around edges, about 30 minutes. Stir to break up the ice crystals. Continue freezing, stirring the mixture every 20 minutes, until it is slushy, about 1 hour. *Makes 1 quart; serves 4*

Desserts & Complements

Grandma's Gelato Cake

Grandma's Gelato Cake, or torta gelato della nonna, is a good
way to use leftover gelato. It's also a great do-ahead dessert—use two or three
of your favorite flavors and freeze them for next weekend.

1 cup Peach Sorbetto (page 72)

1 cup Vanilla Gelato (page 35)

1 cup Strawberry Sorbetto (page 66)

1^1/$_2$ cups heavy cream

^{1}/$_2$ pint fresh raspberries, washed, for garnish

Spread a 1-inch layer of peach sorbetto into a chilled 9-inch
springform pan. Pack firmly. Top with a 1-inch layer of vanilla
gelato, packing firmly. Top vanilla layer with a 1-inch layer of
strawberry sorbetto, packing firmly and smoothing the top. Cover
with plastic wrap and freeze overnight.

   In a deep bowl, beat the cream until soft peaks form. To
unmold the cake, loosen the edges with a sharp knife, then
release the sides. Garnish with the whipped cream and raspberries. *Serves 8*

Duomo

The duomo, or dome, is molded in the colors of the Italian flag.
It is an elegant presentation when served on a pool of Raspberry or
Kiwi Sauce (page 104) or Crema Inglese (page 105).

2 cups Pistachio Gelato (page 43)

2 cups Vanilla Gelato (page 35)

2 cups Raspberry Sorbetto (page 71)

In a chilled 8-cup dome mold, spread a 1-inch layer of pistachio gelato. Pack firmly. Cover with a 1-inch layer of vanilla gelato, packing firmly. Finish by filling with a third layer of raspberry sorbetto, packing firmly and smoothing the top. Cover with plastic wrap and freeze overnight.

To unmold, loosen the edges with a sharp knife, cover with the serving platter, invert both, and remove the mold. To slice, dip a sharp knife in hot water, wipe it dry, then cut each slice.

Serves 8

Cherry Cup

This dish would also be delicious with Custard Gelato (page 55). Fresh cherries are the best,
but when they are not in season, 1 cup (8 ounces) dried cherries can be substituted.

3/4 cup apple juice

3/4 cup spring water

1/2 cup sugar

1/2 teaspoon grated lemon zest

1/2 teaspoon ground cinnamon

1 pound (about 3 cups)
dark sweet cherries, pitted

Vanilla Gelato (page 35)

Chill 6 individual serving dishes until ready to serve.

In a medium saucepan, combine the apple juice, water, sugar, lemon zest, and cinnamon. Bring to a boil, stirring to dissolve the sugar. Add the cherries and reduce heat to a simmer. Cook for 8 to 10 minutes, or until cherries are soft. Let cool to room temperature before serving.

Place a scoop of vanilla gelato into each chilled serving dish. Spoon the cherries and their liquid on top. *Serves 6*

Brioche

Here is a delicious eggy breakfast bread, perfect for accompanying sorbetto on a hot summer morning.

A nice variation is to knead in 1/2 cup raisins soaked in 1/4 cup rum, just before the last rise.

1 package active dry yeast

1 1/2 cups warm milk (105° to 115°F)

1/2 cup sugar plus 1 tablespoon sugar

2 tablespoons extra virgin olive oil

2 egg yolks

4 1/2 to 5 cups unbleached all-purpose flour

1/2 teaspoon salt

1 egg white

In a large bowl, dissolve the yeast in the warm milk. Stir in 1 tablespoon of the 1/2 cup sugar and the olive oil. Set aside until foamy, about 10 minutes.

Whisk the egg yolks into the yeast mixture until well blended. Whisk in 1 cup of the flour, the rest of the 1/2 cup of sugar, and the salt. Cover with plastic wrap and let stand in a warm place for 1 hour.

Whisk in the remaining flour 1/2 cup at a time, switching to a wooden spoon when necessary, until too stiff to stir. Turn the dough onto a floured work surface and knead until smooth, about 5 minutes, adding more flour 1 tablespoon at a time as necessary if the dough is sticky.

Place the dough in a lightly oiled bowl and turn the dough to coat it. Cover the bowl with plastic wrap and let the dough rise in a warm place until doubled, about 1 hour.

Divide the dough into 12 portions, shaping each into a ball. Place each ball in a muffin cup and let rise in a warm place until doubled, about 1 hour.

Preheat the oven to 375°F. In a small bowl, whisk the egg white and sugar just until the sugar is dissolved. Set aside.

Bake the rolls for 18 to 20 minutes, or until golden. Remove from the oven and brush with the egg white mixture while still warm. Let cool in the pan.

To serve, slice in half and fill with a scoop of sorbetto.

Makes 1 dozen rolls

In Sicily, the steamy
heat of morning offers an
excellent excuse to start
eating gelato early. It is
traditional to have a
fresh brioche with a fruit
sorbetto or coffee granita.

The frozen dessert
can be eaten from a dish
with a spoon or scooped
into the split brioche.

Tiramisù

Taking a cue from a favorite Italian dessert, this dessert combines

mascarpone gelato and ladyfingers infused with espresso syrup. Creamy, freshly made gelato is easiest

to work with, or let a previously made batch soften slightly before using.

24–30 *saviordi* (ladyfingers)

2 cups freshly brewed espresso, cooled

4 tablespoons sugar

4 tablespoons dark rum

1½ quarts Mascarpone Gelato (page 35)

1 cup heavy cream

4 ounces bittersweet chocolate, finely chopped

In a 9-inch baking dish, arrange a single layer of ladyfingers. In a medium bowl, combine the espresso, sugar, and rum. Pour the mixture over the ladyfingers to cover. Set aside to soak for 10 to 15 minutes.

In parfait glasses, alternate layers of the soaked cookies and the gelato. Place the layered parfait glasses in the freezer for at least 20 minutes to allow the tiramisù to firm up.

In a deep bowl, beat the cream until soft peaks form. To serve, top the tiramisù with whipped cream and sprinkles of the chopped chocolate. *Serves 8*

Pan di Spagna

In Italy, the preferred flour for this sponge cake is Tipo 00, a wheat flour slightly lower in protein than our all-purpose flour. In her book "The Italian Baker," Carol Field recommends using 1 part pastry flour to 3 parts all-purpose flour to approximate Tipo 00 flour. The addition of the softer flour further lightens the texture of this airy cake.

3 eggs, separated

1/2 teaspoon vanilla extract

1 cup sugar

Pinch of salt

6 tablespoons unbleached all-purpose flour

2 tablespoons pastry flour

1/4 teaspoon baking powder

Preheat the oven to 350°F. Line a 9 by 13-inch sided baking sheet (a jelly roll pan) with parchment paper. Lightly butter the parchment and the sides of the pan.

In a large bowl, with an electric mixer, blend the egg yolks and vanilla together. Add 1/2 cup of the sugar and beat until light and creamy.

In a large bowl, with an electric mixer, beat the egg whites with the salt until frothy. Gradually beat in the remaining 1/2 cup sugar until soft peaks form.

Stir one-third of the beaten egg whites into the egg yolk, then gently fold in the remaining egg whites. Fold the dry ingredients into the egg mixture in 3 increments, taking care not to overmix the batter. Pour into the prepared pan and gently smooth the surface. Bake until the top is firm but not browned, 20 to 25 minutes. Loosen the edges with a knife and invert the cake onto a wire rack. Let cool slightly before removing the parchment paper. *Makes one 9 by 13-inch cake*

Zuccotto

Tuscans claim zuccotto as their invention, first made by the Florentine architect Buontalenti in the 1500s.

Zuccotto can be made ahead and frozen; let it stand in the refrigerator for 30 minutes before serving.

Pan di Spagna (page 94)

4 tablespoons maraschino liqueur

2 cups heavy cream

$1/2$ cup sugar

$1/4$ cup candied orange peel

6 ounces bittersweet chocolate, finely chopped

Cut the pan di Spagna into $1/4$-inch-thick slices and line a 6-cup smooth-sided bowl with them, cutting wedges as needed to fill in the spaces. Drizzle the cake evenly with 1 tablespoon of the maraschino liqueur.

In a deep bowl, whip 1 cup of the cream until soft peaks form. Gradually beat in the sugar and continue to beat until stiff peaks form. Divide the whipped cream among 3 bowls. Fold half of the candied orange peel into one, fold half of the chopped chocolate into another, and leave one plain.

Spoon the orange peel whipped cream into the cake-lined bowl. Arrange a layer of pan di Spagna slices over the top and drizzle evenly with 1 tablespoon of the maraschino.

Spoon the plain whipped cream over the cake and sprinkle with half of the remaining candied orange peel and chopped chocolate, reserving the rest for garnish. Top with a layer of pan di Spagna slices and drizzle evenly with 1 tablespoon of the maraschino.

Spoon in the chocolate whipped cream to fill the mold. Cover the top of the zuccotto with the remaining slices of pan di Spagna, and drizzle evenly with the remaining 1 tablespoon of maraschino. Cover and refrigerate for at least 2 hours or overnight.

To serve, dip the mold in hot water. Invert it onto a serving platter and remove the mold. In a deep bowl, beat the remaining 1 cup cream until soft peaks form. Decorate the zuccotto with the whipped cream and the reserved candied orange peel and chopped chocolate. *Serves 8*

Caramel Semifreddo

Adding whipped cream to a gelato base keeps it from freezing solid, hence the name semifreddo, or "partly chilled."

1¹/₂ cups milk

¹/₂ cup spring water

³/₄ cup sugar

2 large eggs

4 large egg yolks

1¹/₂ cups heavy cream

1 cup crushed amaretti cookies
(about 15 to 20 cookies)

In a small pan, heat the milk over medium heat until bubbles form around the edges of the pan. Cover and set aside. In a medium saucepan, heat the water and ¹/₄ cup of the sugar over medium heat, stirring until the sugar dissolves. Continue to cook until the mixture turns a rich caramel color. Stir in the hot milk. Set the pan in a larger pan of hot water to keep the caramel warm.

In a blender or food processor, beat the remaining ¹/₂ cup sugar and the eggs and egg yolks together until very thick. With the machine running, gradually add half of the hot caramel mixture. Return the mixture to the saucepan. Cover and refrigerate the remaining caramel, reserving it for sauce.

Cook over medium heat, stirring constantly with a wooden spoon, for 6 to 8 minutes, or until the mixture thickens slightly and coats the back of the spoon. Remove from the heat and place it in a bowl of ice water. Stir for 2 minutes to cool the mixture. Cover and refrigerate for at least 2 hours, or until thoroughly chilled. At the same time, refrigerate an 8-cup terrine or eight 1-cup ramekins.

In a deep bowl, beat the cream until soft peaks form. Fold the whipped cream into the custard. Pour half of the mixture into the chilled terrine or ramekins. Sprinkle with half of the amaretti crumbs. Pour in the remaining mixture and smooth. Cover with plastic wrap and freeze overnight.

To unmold, dip the terrine or ramekins into a pan of warm water for a few seconds. Cover with a serving plate, invert both, and remove the terrine or ramekins. Drizzle with the remaining caramel sauce, sprinkle with the remaining amaretti crumbs, and serve at once. *Serves 8*

Chocolate Soufflé Semifreddo

When molded in individual serving dishes, these frozen soufflés resemble their baked cousins.

This recipe can also be made in an 8-cup mold and cut into individual servings.

1 1/2 cups milk

6 ounces semisweet chocolate,
coarsely chopped

2/3 cup sugar

4 large egg yolks

2 cups heavy cream

In a medium saucepan, heat the milk over medium heat until bubbles form around the edges of the pan. Add the chopped chocolate and stir until melted.

In a blender or food processor, beat the sugar and egg yolks together until very thick. With the machine running, gradually add the chocolate-milk mixture. Return the mixture to the saucepan.

Cook over medium heat, stirring constantly with a wooden spoon, for 6 to 8 minutes, or until the mixture thickens slightly and coats the back of the spoon. Remove the pan from the heat and set it in a bowl of ice water. Stir for 2 minutes to cool the mixture. Cover and refrigerate for at least 2 hours, or until thoroughly chilled. At the same time, refrigerate eight 1-cup ramekins.

In a deep bowl, beat the cream until soft peaks form. Fold the cream into the custard mixture. Divide the mixture among the chilled ramekins. Cover with plastic wrap and freeze overnight.

To unmold, dip the ramekins briefly into a pan of hot water and loosen the edges with a sharp knife. Cover each with an individual serving dish, invert both, and remove the mold. Serve at once. *Serves 8*

Brutti Ma Buoni

Ugly, but good. These macaroonlike cookies keep well in an airtight container,

and are a delicious accompaniment to gelati.

3 cups (20 ounces) slivered almonds, toasted and finely chopped (see page 106)

2 cups sugar

7 egg whites

Preheat the oven to 325°F. Line a baking sheet with parchment paper.

In a large bowl, stir the almonds and sugar together and set aside.

In a large bowl, beat the egg whites until stiff peaks form. Fold them into the sugar mixture.

Drop spoonfuls on the prepared pan and bake for 35 to 40 minutes, or until golden brown. *Makes about 3 dozen cookies*

Chocolate Meringue Kisses

This recipe makes a lot of sweet little kisses to top gelato or sorbetto, but they will keep for days in an airtight container.

The meringue can also be piped into a flat disk of any size, which can be used for serving gelato.

6 tablespoons unsweetened cocoa powder

1 cup confectioners' sugar

8 egg whites

1/2 teaspoon fresh lemon juice

1 cup granulated sugar

Preheat the oven to 250°F. Line 2 baking sheets with parchment paper and set aside.

Sift the cocoa and confectioners' sugar together into a medium bowl.

In a large bowl, beat the egg whites with the lemon juice until soft peaks form. Beat in 3 tablespoons of the granulated sugar. Beat until stiff, then beat in the remaining sugar, beating until glossy peaks form.

Gently fold the cocoa mixture into the beaten egg whites. Place the mixture in a pastry bag fitted with a plain tip with at least a 1/2-inch opening. Pipe 1-inch "kisses" onto the lined pans.

Bake in the oven for 2 hours, or until meringues are dry and crisp. Turn off the oven and let meringues dry further in the oven for 2 hours, or overnight if desired. *Makes 4 dozen kisses*

Biscotti di Prato

This popular cookie is famous for dipping into espresso or vin santo. It is a nice, crunchy complement to gelato.

For a variation, try substituting toasted pine nuts for the almonds.

1 cup whole almonds	1/2 teaspoon baking soda
1 3/4 cups cake flour	4 large eggs
1 cup unbleached all-purpose flour	3/4 cup sugar
1 teaspoon salt	2 teaspoons vanilla extract
1 teaspoon baking powder	1 tablespoon grated orange zest

Preheat the oven to 325°F. Line a baking sheet with parchment.

Spread the almonds on another baking sheet and bake for 12 to 15 minutes, or until golden brown. Transfer to a cool surface and let stand until cool.

In a large bowl, mix together the cake flour, all-purpose flour, salt, baking powder, baking soda, and the cooled almonds.

In a medium bowl, beat the eggs and sugar until pale in color. Add the vanilla and orange zest and mix well. Stir the egg mixture into the dry ingredients just until blended. Do not overmix. The dough will be sticky.

Transfer the dough to the prepared baking sheet. Moisten your fingers with water and form the dough into a log about 3 inches wide and 1 inch high. Bake until a toothpick inserted into the center comes out clean, about 30 minutes. Remove to a wire rack to cool to the touch. Reduce the oven temperature to 275°F. Replace the parchment paper on the baking sheet.

Cut the log into 1/2-inch diagonal slices and place them on the pan. Bake for 10 minutes, then turn the cookies. Continue to bake until the cookies are a pale golden brown, about 20 minutes. Transfer to wire racks to cool. *Makes 2 dozen cookies*

Pizzelle Cones or Wafers

If you have a pizzelle iron, you can make your own gelato cones by shaping the pizzelle while warm, or cut them into fans and insert one in the top of each serving of gelato. Other shapes can be made by draping a soft pizzelle over a glass or the neck of a bottle, or pressing it into a muffin cup. Optional flavors can be added, such as nutmeg, cinnamon, or vanilla.

1/2 cup all-purpose flour

1/4 teaspoon baking soda

Pinch of salt

1/2 teaspoon freshly ground nutmeg or
ground cinnamon (optional)

2 egg whites

1/2 cup sugar

4 tablespoons unsalted butter,
melted and cooled

1 teaspoon vanilla (optional)

In a large bowl, combine the flour, baking soda, salt, and optional spices. Stir to mix and set aside.

In a large bowl, beat the egg whites until soft peaks form. Gradually beat in the sugar until stiff, glossy peaks form. Whisk in 2 tablespoons of the melted butter (and optional vanilla, if using). Fold the egg whites into the flour mixture. Place the remaining butter in a container with a pour spout.

Heat a pizzelle iron according to the manufacturer's instructions and brush it with a light coat of the remaining melted butter. Pour a small amount of batter in the center of each pizzelle stamp, close, and cook for 30 to 45 seconds, until golden brown. Shape as desired while warm, or cut into quarters to serve as wafers. Repeat the process to use all the remaining batter. *Makes 6 cones or 24 wafers*

Fruit Sauces

Fresh fruit sauces are the perfect accompaniment to gelato. These easy combinations can be enhanced with the addition of 1 or 2 tablespoons of liqueur such as kirsch, Grand Marnier, or maraschino.

Apricot Sauce

1 pound fresh apricots, peeled and pitted

1/2 cup sugar

1/4 cup spring water

Juice of 1/2 lemon

Raspberry Sauce

2 cups fresh raspberries, washed

2/3 cup sugar

1/4 cup spring water

Juice of 1/2 lemon

Kiwi Sauce

6 fresh kiwis, peeled

3/4 cup sugar

1/4 cup spring water

Juice of 1/2 lemon

For each sauce, combine all the ingredients in a blender or food processor and process until smooth. For a silky sauce, pass the purée through a fine-meshed sieve. *Makes approximately 2 1/2 cups; serves 6*

Crema Inglese

This classic dessert sauce can be varied simply by adding a variety of other flavors to the finished sauce.

The sauce can be made and refrigerated a day ahead of serving.

2 cups whole milk

1 cup heavy cream

1/2 vanilla bean, split lengthwise

4 egg yolks

1/2 cup sugar

In a saucepan, combine the milk, cream, and vanilla bean, scraping the seeds into the milk. Heat over medium heat until bubbles form around the edges of the pan. Set aside and cover.

In a medium bowl, beat the egg yolks and sugar together until pale in color. Remove the vanilla bean from the mixture and gradually whisk the mixture into the eggs.

Return to the saucepan and cook over low heat, stirring constantly, until the custard thickens enough to coat the back of the spoon. Strain through a fine-meshed sieve. Serve warm or chilled. *Makes 3 1/2 cups*

Chocolate Cream Sauce

After straining, return the sauce to the saucepan and add 4 ounces finely chopped bittersweet chocolate, stirring until melted.

Coffee Cream Sauce

Substitute 1/4 cup freshly ground coffee for the vanilla bean.

Orange Cream Sauce

Substitute 1/2 cup fresh orange juice for the vanilla bean. Add 1 teaspoon finely grated orange zest after straining.

Techniques

Peeling Cactus Pears

Many cactus pears purchased in the market have had their stickers mechanically removed, but there are usually still some fine irritating ones remaining. The best way to peel the pears is to slice off 1/4 inch at each end and stick a fork in one end. With a sharp knife, make a slit the length of the pear through the skin. Using the knife, loosen the edge of the slit and flatten the skin against the cutting board, rotating the fruit as you unroll the skin. See page 63 for a photo illustration of this technique.

Toasting Nuts

To toast almonds or walnuts, place them on a baking sheet in a preheated 350°F oven for 8 to 10 minutes, or until golden brown and aromatic. Toast pine nuts at the same temperature for 5 to 7 minutes.

Toasting and Skinning Hazelnuts

Toast the nuts on a baking sheet in a preheated 325°F oven for 10 to 12 minutes, or until aromatic. While the nuts are still hot, place them in a terrycloth towel and rub them together. Most of the brown skins should come off.

Peeling Peaches

Score an X in the skin and drop the peaches in boiling water for 30 seconds. Immediately immerse them in ice water and the skin will slip right off.

Zesting Citrus

Use a citrus zester or grater to grate the brightly colored skin of citrus or remove the skin with a vegetable peeler, then mince it. Do not use the white pith, as it is bitter.

Using Alcohol in Gelato

Too much alcohol can slow or stop the freezing process. Use the following guidelines for each 4 cups of base mixture:

Wine (up to 12 percent alcohol):

less than 1 cup

Dessert wine or liqueur (up to 25 percent alcohol):

up to 1/2 cup

Distilled alcohol (up to 48 percent alcohol):

up to 1/4 cup

Flavor Glossary

Italian	English	Italian	English
Albicocca	Apricot	*Limone*	Lemon
Amarena	Wild cherry	*Mandarino*	Tangerine
Ananas	Pineapple	*Mandorla*	Almond
Arancia	Orange	*Marron glacé*	Candied chestnuts
Bacio	Chocolate with chopped hazelnuts	*Mela*	Apple
Banana	Banana	*Melone*	Melon
Buontalenti	Eggy	*Menta*	Mint
Caffè	Coffee	*Miele*	Honey
Canela	Cinnamon	*Mirtillo*	Blueberry
Caramel	Caramel	*Mora*	Blackberry
Cassata siciliana	Contains bits of dried fruit	*Nocciola*	Hazelnut
Castagna	Chestnut	*Noce*	Walnut
Ciliegia	Cherry	*Panna*	Whipped cream
Cioccolato	Chocolate	*Pera*	Pear
Cioccolato bianco	White chocolate	*Pesca*	Peach
Cocco	Coconut	*Pescanoce*	Nectarine
Cocomero	Watermelon	*Pistacchio*	Pistachio
Crema	Custard	*Pompelmo*	Grapefruit
Datteri	Dates	*Prugna*	Plum
Fico	Fig	*Ribes*	Currants
Fico d'India	Cactus pear	*Riso*	Rice
Fior di latte	Pure, rich milk and sugar	*Rosa*	Rose
Fior di panna	Pure, rich cream and sugar	*Stracciatella*	Vanilla with fine chocolate pieces
Fragola	Strawberry	*Tarocchio*	Blood orange
Fragoline	Wild strawberries	*Tartufo*	Chocolate truffle
Frutti di bosco	Wild berries	*Torrone*	Nougat
Gelsomino	Jasmine	*Uva*	Grape
Gianduia	Chocolate-hazelnut	*Vaniglia*	Vanilla
Lampone	Raspberry		

Resources

Supplies

Chef's Catalog
P.O. Box 620048
Dallas, TX 75262
Tel. (800) 338-3232
Fax (800) 967-3291
www.chefscatalog.com
Ice cream makers

Hayward Enterprises
Perfect Puree Company
975 Vintage Avenue
St. Helena, CA 94574
Tel. (707) 967-8700
Fax (707) 967-8799
California white peach purée

Manicaretti Imports
5332 College Avenue, No. 200
Oakland, CA 94618
Tel. (800) 799-9830
Saba, chestnut honey

Sur La Table
Stores nationwide
Catalogue Tel. (800) 243-0852
Ice cream makers

Williams-Sonoma
Stores nationwide
Catalogue Tel. (800) 541-2233
Ice cream makers

Gelaterie

Sicily

Mondello
Gelateria Antico Chiosco (page 14)
Piazza Mondello
Beachfront resort near Palermo

Noto
Corrado Costanzo (page 14)
Via Silvio Spaventa, 7/9

Palermo
Umberto and Giovanni Stancampiano
Gelateria Stancampiano (pages 15–16)
Via Notarbartolo, 51

Piedmont

Alessandria
Claudio and Enrico Elli
Cremeria del Corso (pages 21–25)
Corso Roma, 69

Tuscany

Campi Bisenzio
Guido Ballerini
Il Fantino Gelateria-Latteria (pages 18–21)
Via 24 Maggio, 12

Firenze
Piero Vivoli
Il Gelato Vivoli (page 21)
Via Isola delle Stinche, 7/r

Antonio Lisciandro
Gelateria Carabe (pages 16–18, 62–63)
Via Ricasoli, 60/r

Forte dei Marmi
Antonio Lisciandro
Gelateria Carabe (pages 16–18)
Via PI Carrara
Vittoria Apuana

Livorno
Antonio Bartoletti
Dai Dai Gelateria Artigiana (pages 24–27)
Via del Sorriso, 8 Fraz.
Castiglioncello

Pelago
Giancarlo Sottani
Gelateria Sottani (page 35)
Via Forlivese, 93
Località San Francesco

Bibliography

Caviezel, Luca. *Scienza e technologia del gelato artigianale*. Pinerolo (TO): Chiriotti, 1996.

Gosetti, Fernanda. *Il Gelato*. Milano: Fabbri, 1985.

Landra, Laura and Margherita. *Come fare i gelati in casa*. Milano: De Vecchi, 1997.

Preti, G. *Il gelato artigianale italiani*. Milano: Hoepli, 1982.

Acknowledgments

Pamela Sheldon Johns would like to thank two dear friends, Lucy De Fazio and Kimberly Wicks Bartolozzi, for their invaluable help with research and logistics in Italy.

Thanks also to Antonio Davì, president of the Messina, Sicily, convivium of Slow Food for spending a day with me in Palermo. Much appreciation back at home to my friends who helped with recipe testing and other details: Judy Dawson, Philippa Farrar, Mari Kay Bartoli, and especially Gioia Bartoli Cardi.

Alaia and I wish to express our appreciation and love to our traveling companions, Donna LeBlanc and Linda Hale. Kisses to Courtney, who never once complained about tasting so many *gelati!* Tremendous thanks and appreciation to the generous collaboration of Jennifer Barry, a great partner and friend.

Jennifer Barry Design would like to thank the following individuals and establishments for their support of this book project:

Ten Speed publisher Kirsty Melville and editorial director Lorena Jones for their continued editorial guidance and enthusiasm for Italian cuisine; Joyce Oudkerk-Pool for traveling to Italy to photograph all the wonderful *gelaterie* that we may now enjoy in this book. For this, in addition to Joyce's lovely photography of the recipes with the help of stylist Pouké, who has styled every book in our Italian food series so beautifully, we are most appreciative; Kristen Wurz, Leslie Barry, Carolyn Miller, Barbara King, and prop stylist Carol Hacker for their expert assistance in producing the book. Special thanks go to Jeannie and Gary Rulli of Emporio Rulli in Larkspur, California, for inspiring both our photography and our taste buds with their authentic *gelati* and *dolci*. And to Pamela Sheldon Johns, our muse and friend on another culinary adventure to our favorite country, our greatest appreciation of her talent and inspiration for another delicious book together.

Recipe Index

General Index